GET SMART ABOUT
MICHELLE
OBAMA

Adam Kent

GET SMART ABOUT MICHELLE OBAMA

**R CKET
BOOKS**

Get Smart about Michelle Obama
by Adam Kent

Published by Rocket Books, Inc.
New York, NY, USA

Copyright © 2023 Rocket Books, Inc.

All rights reserved. No portion of this book may be reproduced in any form without permission from the publisher, except as permitted by U.S. copyright law. For permissions contact:
info@rocketkidsbookclub.com

Disclaimer: Please note the information contained within this document is for educational and entertainment purposes only. All effort has been executed to present accurate, up to date, and reliable, complete information. No warranties of any kind are declared or implied. The content within this book has been derived from different sources. By reading this document the reader agrees that under no circumstances is the author responsible for any losses, direct or indirect, which are incurred as a result of the use of information contained within the document, including, but not limited to, - errors, commissions, or inaccuracies.

ADAM KENT

For kids...
who dream big,
who work hard to become better,
who get up when they fall,
who know we are all human and
all worthy of respect and success.

For my son Little Adam...
who lights up my life.

May your dreams come true.

This book is for you.

GET SMART ABOUT MICHELLE OBAMA

ABOUT THIS BOOK

This biography book is meant to be a fun, brief and inspirational look at the life of a famous person. Reading biographies can help learn from people who have experienced extraordinary things. While you read through the books in this series, think about how their experiences can help you in your own life!

As you read this book you will find bolded words. There are definitions of the words at the end of each page. You will also find interesting facts at the end of each chapter. Plus, there are some questions to get you thinking at the end of the book.

I hope you enjoy learning about this extraordinary person!

Have a great time reading,

Adam Kent

CONTENTS

AT A GLANCE 11
FAST FACTS 13
1: THE EARLY DAYS 15
   FUN FACTS 22
2: FAMILY MATTERS 25
   FUN FACTS 33
3: A UNIQUE EDUCATION 35
   FUN FACTS 39
4: A CAREER TO REMEMBER 41
   FUN FACTS 55
5: HOBBIES & PASSIONS 59
   FUN FACTS 64
6: A PERSONAL LIFE 67
   FUN FACTS 72
7: A LASTING LEGACY 73
INSPIRATIONAL QUOTES 77
BOOK DISCUSSION 87

GLOSSARY **91**
SELECTED REFERENCES................... **97**

ADAM KENT

GET SMART ABOUT
MICHELLE OBAMA

Adam Kent

GET SMART ABOUT MICHELLE OBAMA

MICHELLE OBAMA
AT A GLANCE

Michelle Obama, the 44th First Lady of the United States from 2009-2017, is a lawyer, author, and role model. She spearheaded the "Let's Move!" campaign during her time in the White House, promoting healthier lifestyles for kids. Her memoir "Becoming" is a bestseller, tracing her life's path from Chicago to the White House. Michelle champions education, veterans, and equality. Her powerful speeches and activism inspire individuals of all ages to engage in meaningful change. Exploring her journey offers insights into leadership, activism, and the power of determination.

MICHELLE OBAMA
FAST FACTS

1. Michelle Obama was the First Lady of the United States of America from 2009-2017.

2. She was born in Chicago, Illinois, in 1964.

3. She studied at a university called Princeton as an undergraduate and received her law degree from Harvard Law School in 1988.

4. As First Lady she was committed to health and wellness causes.

5. She has two children with Barack Obama, who was President of the United States.

CHAPTER 1
THE EARLY DAYS

Michelle Obama was born in Chicago, Illinois, on January 17, 1964. Her birth name is Michelle LaVaughn Robinson. She grew up in a household with both of her parents, as well as her sibling, Craig, who was just less than two years older than Michelle.

When Michelle was a child, her family lived in a small, modest home on the south side of Chicago in an area called Calumet City. Their house was so modest that Michelle and her brother didn't have their own room. In fact, they slept in the living room. They used a sheet to divide the space so that they both had a little privacy.

The Robinson family made the best of the **humble** apartment. They remained a close-knit family despite the somewhat challenging living arrangement. Throughout Michelle's childhood, they spent a lot of quality time together as a family. They made it a point to eat

---

humble /ˈhəmbəl/ adjective 1: not regarding others as inferior 2: expressed without too much pride 3: low in condition or rank *<example: humble beginnings>*

a lot of family meals together. They played and read together. Michelle was also very close to her brother, Craig. They were friends and spent a lot of time playing together.

Michelle's father was a hard worker who worked for the city. He was also a community activist and a leader of a local political party. He was a neighborhood captain of the Democratic party.

Michelle's mother initially worked at a local department store as a secretary when the kids were very young. However, she really wanted to be with the kids to raise them, so she eventually quit her job. She then spent much of their youth as a stay-at-home mother. She wanted to be able to focus on raising her children how she felt was best.

During her early childhood years, Michelle's family placed a great **emphasis** on education with the kids. Reading was encouraged very early on, so the kids were able to read at a young age. They both could read at just four years old, which is exceptional. In addition to reading a lot, the kids worked hard at school. In fact, both Michelle and her older brother skipped second grade entirely. This was partly because their mother bought math and reading workbooks and had

---

emphasis /ˈemfəsəs/ noun: a force that is given to something that is spoken or written to draw attention to it <example: *a special emphasis on learning*>

them working on them in their free time.

Their mother also encouraged both children to be hard workers and disciplined. When they were kids, she would assign them tasks and chores. She expected that they would be completed well. She also encouraged them to speak their mind and express themselves freely. This all helped them reach the success they had later.

In middle school, starting in sixth grade to be exact, Michelle was placed in her school's gifted program. She remained in it until high school. While she was in the program, she took French classes and was placed in advanced science classes as well.

For high school, Michelle went to a special school called a magnet school. Magnet schools are schools that have a specific focus that draws students from different areas interested in attending. The high school Michelle attended was a magnet school for gifted children called Whitney M. Young Magnet High School. This was quite an accomplishment for the family!

Sports were also a big part of Michelle's childhood. She and her brother were so close in age that they were friends and played together throughout childhood. Michelle kept up with her brother and played along with many of the things he did when he was young, which included sports. They both became great at sports. Michelle's brother later, in college, excelled so much that he was named Ivy League Player of the Year in two different years. He even almost earned a position in the National Basketball Association (NBA) as a professional basketball player!

    Looking back on the childhood of Michelle Obama, you can see that the inspiration and careful upbringing by her parents, as well as the closeness and love shared amongst the family, created a great foundation for the later success that Michelle and her brother earned. For the Robinsons, hard work paid off!

CHAPTER 1
FUN FACTS

1. The city of Chicago is where Michelle Obama was born. It is in Illinois. Chicago is the third largest city in the whole United States.

2. Chicago is the place where the atom was first split. This happened at the University of Chicago, in 1942.

3. Chicago is known to be the birthplace of the world's first brownie! According to the known record, it was made at the Palmer Hotel in Chicago in 1893.

4. The world's first backwards running river is in the city of Chicago. The river is called the Chicago River. This river was engineered to flow away from Lake Michigan in order to help prevent sewage from entering into the lake. Lake Michigan is a freshwater lake.

GET SMART ABOUT MICHELLE OBAMA

CHAPTER 2
FAMILY MATTERS

Michelle Obama's upbringing was shaped by her close-knit family – her parents, Fraser Robinson III and Marian Shields Robinson, and her older brother, Craig Robinson. Their influence and values played a significant role in shaping her character, aspirations, and commitment to positive change.

Michelle lived with her parents while growing up. Michelle's father,

Fraser Robinson III, was a key figure in her early life. He worked as a city water plant employee in Chicago, displaying a strong work ethic that left a lasting impression on Michelle. He was also an activist in the community and participated in politics with the local Democratic party as a neighborhood captain.

As a father, Fraser was thoughtful about the future. He used to take the family driving around a wealthy neighborhood in Chicago near their home called Pill Hill to help the children see what education and hard work could lead to. At the same time, he cautioned the children against spending too much on material things. He told his children that they wouldn't want to become "house poor." To him this meant that it wasn't smart to spend your money on material things like a big fancy house, but then not have enough saved to be able to have the freedom to do the things you want, especially in case of emergency. So, it is better to have a smaller house and more savings, so that you can do more outside of the house and have more choices.

Fraser was a hard worker and a great father. Unfortunately, for the family, during his thirties, he developed a disease called Multiple Sclerosis. Multiple Sclerosis is a **debilitating** disease that he

---

debilitating /di-'bi-lə-ˌtā-tiŋ/ noun: a force that is given to something that is spoken or written to draw attention to it <example: *a debilitating fear*>

ultimately died from when Michelle was still young and just in her twenties.

Before he died, Michelle's dad continued to work even though he suffered from pain and disability. He worked and worked until he just couldn't work anymore. The family would observe Fraser walking to work many days with two canes. He hardly missed a day of work. Even though things took longer for him, he knew what he needed to do to take care of his family. In turn, Michelle's family saw him as their hero.

The example of Fraser's persistence and dedication to working despite pain and challenge served as a great example to Michelle and her brother. Fraser

Robinson has always been a source of inspiration for Michelle Obama.

Michelle's mother was named Marian Shields Robinson. When Michelle was young, Marian worked as a secretary at a local department store called Spiegel's. But Michelle's mother really wanted to devote a lot of focus and attention to raising her children and teaching them the values she thought would be good for their future success.

Michelle's mother decided to quit her job in order to work as a stay-at-home mom. She tried hard to teach the great values of hard work and discipline by giving her children a lot of chores and extra work. These chores taught them responsibility. This is an important quality to have.

Her mother also **cultivated** a close bond and loving relationship in the family with family dinners and quality time spent together. She taught free speech, by allowing the kids to voice their opinions and concerns freely and with acceptance.

Michelle has one sibling, a brother, named Craig. Michelle and her brother have always been close. Craig excelled as a kid like did Michelle. He also has become successful as an adult. He excelled at sports throughout his youth and

---

cultivate /ˈkəl-tə-ˌvāt/ verb: to raise and help grow with work and attention <*example: cultivate corn or cultivate a friendship*>

also, all throughout school and university. As an adult, he became a basketball coach at a couple of major universities in the United States. As of 2022, Craig held a top position with a title of Executive Director at National Association of Basketball Coaches.

The lessons learned from each member of Michelle's early family helped inspire her into the leader she became. Her father Fraser's work ethic, her mother Marian's community involvement, and her brother Craig's supportive sibling bond formed the basis for Michelle's commitment to education, public service, and equality. Her upbringing reminds us that the family unit can play a central role in cultivating character, values, and dreams that pave the way for our future path toward making a meaningful impact on the world.

CHAPTER 2
FUN FACTS

1. Michelle Obama has a brother Craig who is quite tall. His height is six feet and six inches. The world average height of a male is five feet and six inches.

2. Michelle's brother Craig was a basketball player and then a basketball coach. Basketball originated in the United States in 1891 in Massachusetts.

3. Michelle's mom used to make her birthday cakes every year growing up.

4. One of Michelle's favorite memories of her family growing up was the vacations they took in Michigan at a place called "Duke's Happy Holiday Resort."

CHAPTER 3
A UNIQUE EDUCATION

Michelle Obama's journey through higher education was marked by dedication, hard work, and a commitment to excellence. It was all of these things that enabled her to get into the best schools in the United States. And that education at Princeton University and Harvard Law School shaped her into the influential leader she would later become.

In 1981, Michelle started at Princeton University campus as a freshman. She followed her brother Craig's lead. He also went to Princeton. Determined to excel, she pursued a major in sociology and a minor in African American studies. Michelle's academic journey was marked by her strong work ethic and intellectual curiosity.

Michelle was also committed to social justice and equality. She was an active member of the Third World Center, which aimed to create a sense of community for students of color. She also took part in the Organization of African Unity, where she collaborated with fellow students to promote awareness about African culture and history.

In 1985, Michelle graduated college, *cum laude*, which means "with honors". She did so well she was awarded a special **designation** to recognize her success.

After graduating from Princeton, Michelle continued her educational journey at Harvard Law School. In 1985, she entered this school known for producing top legal minds. At Harvard, Michelle's passion for learning and advocating for justice only grew. Her academic achievements were notable, earning her a place on the editorial board of the

---

designation /ˌde-zig-ˈnā-shən/ noun 1: an act of choosing to do something *<example: designation of protected land>* 2: a title or name that identifies something

Harvard Law Review.

Michelle's commitment to public service also shone through her involvement in the Harvard Legal Aid Bureau. This organization provided legal assistance to those in need. Her dedication to advocacy and supporting less fortunate communities remained a driving force throughout her college years. Michelle graduated from Harvard Law School with a law degree in 1988.

CHAPTER 3
FUN FACTS

1. In college Michelle Obama studied Sociology before she became a lawyer. Sociology is the study of how people relate to other people. It also includes the study of the behavior of people in groups too, such as families and communities.

2. Michelle Obama went to Harvard Law School. Harvard Law School is one of the best law schools in the world. It is also the oldest current law school in the United States. It

was opened in 1817. That was over 200 years ago!

CHAPTER 4
A CAREER TO REMEMBER

Michelle Obama is famous for being First Lady of the United States. Before meeting and marrying Barack Obama, who later became the President, Michelle Obama had a successful career.

Michelle Obama's success during college continued

immediately after graduating from Harvard Law School with a law degree in 1988. Michelle started working shortly after in a law firm that had an office in Chicago called Sidley Austin.

A couple of years after working for Sidley Austin, Michelle changed career directions and moved from **corporate** law into public service. In 1991, Michelle got a job working as an assistant for the mayor of Chicago, who was at the time, Mayor Richard Daley. It was a big honor working for the mayor so soon after graduating law school!

---

corporate /ˈkȯr-p(ə-)rət/ adjective: relating to corporations, which are businesses that have been given by law that title and the rights that go with it <*example: corporate America*>

After working for the mayor, Michelle continued working for the City of Chicago in planning and development. In 1993, Michelle continued the exciting pace of her career and took a position at the head of an organization called the Chicago Office of Public Allies. This organization was a non-profit devoted to helping to train young people to become leaders in their community and develop successful careers in public service. Michelle spent a few years in this position.

In 1996, Michelle changed positions again. She then started working at a **prestigious** university

---

prestigious /pre-'sti-jəs/ adjective: to have importance or respect that is earned through excellence <*example: prestigious award*>

in Chicago, the University of Chicago. There, she used her leadership, service skills and experience in a position called the Assistant Dean of Student Services. Following in her father's footsteps as an active community member and leader, in this role, Michelle helped the university develop its first community service program. This program was built to help develop the community and provide services for community members.

After several years as the Assistant Dean at the University of Chicago, Michelle moved on to work for the University of Chicago Hospitals in community relations there. She started as Executive Director, which is a top leadership position, and later was promoted to vice president of community relations at the University of Chicago Medical Center. This is an even higher position. She also worked in a leadership position at the Chicago Council on Global Affairs.

All the positions that Michelle Obama held were exceptional. It was also a great honor for Michelle, as a minority, to reach such great success in so many different important positions in the community and city of Chicago.

By this time, Michelle was already married to Barack Obama. Because she had gained so much experience working for the city in important leadership positions, working in community service, she had gained the perfect experience to help her husband campaign for President of the United States. Michelle travelled around the whole country giving speeches and also making public appearances to help Barack during the time that he was running for president. Michelle also continued in her roles at the University of Chicago and the Chicago Council on Global Affairs part-time all the way until Barack Obama was inaugurated as President of the United States on January 20, 2009.

First Lady of the United States of America

When Barack Obama became president, Michelle Obama took on

the role of First Lady of the United States full-time. In order to help provide her daughters with a sense of **normalcy**, Michelle invited her mother to live at the White House to help raise them and keep them **grounded**, knowing that her role as First Lady would be demanding.

As First Lady of the United States from 2009-2017, Michelle Obama took on some major causes as the focus of her work in the role. Her experience as a child growing up with a mother who really emphasized hard work

---

grounded / ˈgraun-dəd/ adjective: mentally and emotionally stable *<example: a grounded attitude>*

normalcy /ˈnȯr-məl-sē/ noun: the state of being normal or regular *<example: a return to normalcy after a terrible fight>*

and **discipline** helped create her focus in the White House on promoting military service and helping military families. The United States Military is, after all, a form of service that teaches great discipline and hard work.

During her time serving as First Lady, Michelle Obama also spent a lot of time volunteering and serving various communities. She volunteered at homeless shelters and soup kitchens near the White House. She also traveled around to schools giving speeches to thousands of students about the

---

discipline /'di-sə-plən/ noun: control that is gained through practice or insisting that rules be followed <example: *She gained discipline through practice.*> verb 1: punishment 2: a strict training meant to strengthen <example: *Teach discipline to a child.*>

importance of healthy living and volunteering in the community.

As part of her official role, Michelle Obama also focused on healthy living. To lead by example, at the White House, she asked the cooking staff to make healthy meals for her family and visiting guests as well. In addition, she organized an official and public project to plant the first **organic** vegetable garden at the White House with the help of dozens of the local fifth graders from Washington D.C. Near the garden, they also set up many beehives to produce fresh honey, which has

---

organic /ȯr-'ga-nik/ adjective: a type of food or beverage that is produced without the use of artificial chemicals *<example: organic food>* 2: related to living things

great health benefits, and it is healthier than sugar! In 2012, Michelle wrote a book to promote the organic lifestyle and local garden project called *American Grown: The Story of the White House Kitchen Garden and Gardens Across America*.

Michelle took her interest in healthy living to schools across the United States in 2012 as First Lady with a program she called "Let's Move." With the help of athletes around the country, the program was designed to get kids in local communities out and moving and trying new sports and activities in order to stay healthy.

Her work as First Lady shows how committed Michelle Obama was to being a role model to young people across the country. She wanted to lead by example of how to live and eat and move. She also wanted to give tools and lessons to help young people across the country become the best they could be by starting off with healthy habits.

After the White House

In 2018, after serving as First Lady in the White House, Michelle Obama released another book. The book was a memoir, which is a story of someone's life, called "Becoming." She wrote the book to explain how she found her voice and way following a challenging beginning. She also wrote the book in hopes of inspiring young people.

After writing the book, she decided to make an **audio** version of it. Her audio book was so well loved that she received a Grammy award for Best Spoken Word album. Do you believe that? The Grammys are famous music awards, so it may sound unusual, but an audio book is spoken word!

After their roles in the White House, Michelle and Barack also started a production company. This production company was for films. They called it Higher Ground Productions. Soon after, they received **contracts** with the

---

audio /ˈȯ-dē-ˌō/ adjective: relating to sound *<example: audio equipment>*

contract /ˈkän-ˌtrakt/ noun: an agreement, often legal, between two or more people or parties *<example: a work contract>*

popular television streaming service called Netflix. These contracts were given for them so that they could produce a series of documentaries over the course of many years which would then be featured on Netflix.

Their first documentary film, which was called American Factory was released on Netflix in 2019. Critics liked it so much that it received an Academy Award for best **documentary** feature in 2020.

Another documentary was released on Netflix in 2020. This one was called "Becoming." Can you take a guess at what this

---

documentary /ˌdä-kyə-ˈmen-tə-rē/ noun: a film or a book dealing with factual events <example: a documentary on whales>

documentary is about? Well, this documentary was about Michelle Obama's experience promoting her book "Becoming" around the United States on a tour, speaking to young people.

In 2021, after decades of outstanding achievements and professional work, Michelle Obama was **inducted** into the National Women's Hall of Fame. This is an institution created in 1969 by men in New York to honor great women of the United States. Since it opened, there have been just under three hundred women inducted into the Hall of Fame as of 2022, including Michelle Obama!

---

induct /in-'dəkt/ verb: to admit as a member
<example: a induct into the Hall of Fame>

CHAPTER 4
FUN FACTS

1. The *first* First Lady of the United States was Martha Washington. She was married to the *first* President of the United States, who was George Washington. Martha Washington served as first lady from 1789 to 1797.

2. Organic food products usually contain less pesticides that can be harmful to people. Organic produce, such as fruits and vegetables are made without pesticides and are also frequently found to be higher in nutrients that are

healthy for people than produce that isn't organic.

3. Only a few of the First Ladies have grown ever vegetable gardens at the White House. On record, there are a total of three: Eleanor Roosevelt, Hilary Clinton, and Michelle Obama. Eleanor Roosevelt called hers the Victory Garden and used it to promote growing one's own vegetables during a time when food was harder to get. Hilary Clinton planted her vegetable garden on the White House roof! Michelle Obama made her vegetable garden much larger than any other First Ladies

before.

4. Netflix is a television service that allows a user to stream movies and TV shows for a small monthly fee or subscription. As of 2022 there are about 220 million subscribers for Netflix.

GET SMART ABOUT MICHELLE OBAMA

CHAPTER 5
HOBBIES AND PASSIONS

Michelle Obama has many hobbies and passions that are geared toward self-improvement and wellness. She likes to keep moving and keep improving, even when she is sitting!

One of her favorite hobbies is knitting. of her adult life to community service in some way. She thinks that it's important to take moments to have silence and peace and that the calm that knitting provides is healthy. She also thinks that knitting is a nice want to produce something in an act that has a clean beginning and a clean ending and is useful!

Michelle Obama is also a fitness enthusiast. To just keep moving she exercises regularly. Her favorite sport is tennis.

Michelle is also a person that likes to encourage others and give back. She worked in community service after college and has continued since. Her **charity** work took center stage too during her

---

charity /ˈkän-ˌtrakt/ noun 1: an organization focused on helping people in need <example: donated to a charity> 2: a gift intended to help people 3: goodwill toward people youth to get outdoors and exercise and stay healthy.

years as First Lady at the White House. She spent her time in that role volunteering at homeless shelters and soup kitchens. She also started the Let's Move initiative to inspire America's youth to be active and healthy.

In 2014, Michelle and Barack Obama also started the Obama Foundation, which is based in Chicago. The Obama Foundation is a nonprofit organization created by former President Barack Obama and Michelle Obama. It aims to help people, especially young ones, become leaders and bring positive changes to their communities and the world.

The foundation has programs like the Obama Scholars, which support young leaders by providing them with education and connections to help them make a bigger impact. They're like a team of future leaders working together.

The Obama Foundation is also building the Obama Presidential Center, a place where people can learn about history and get inspired to make a difference. The foundation's My Brother's Keeper Alliance helps young boys and men of color get the same chances as others. And the Girls Opportunity Alliance helps girls around the world get a good education.

Through events and discussions, the Obama Foundation brings people together to share ideas and find solutions to important problems. It's a way for everyone, including kids, to be part of making the world a better place.

CHAPTER 5
FUN FACTS

1. The Obama Foundation helps young people by providing them with scholarships. A scholarship is a gift of financial help given to a student who qualifies that is meant to help them further their education. There are scholarships available for high school, college and school after college. There are many ways a student can qualify for scholarships, so it is a good idea to learn about the types of scholarships you may be able to qualify for and how to

qualify for ones available to you.

2. Charitable organizations rely on donations from people. Most of the money, about 70%, that charities receive come from individuals.

3. December is the month of the year when the most donations are made.

GET SMART ABOUT MICHELLE OBAMA

CHAPTER 6
A PERSONAL LIFE

By now you know that Michelle Obama is famously married to Barack Obama, the 44th President of the United States. Would you like to know how they met?

Michelle and Barack met right after Michelle graduated Harvard Law School during her first job at the law firm in Chicago at a law firm called Sidley Austin. Michelle worked there for a while before Barack Obama did.

Michelle and Barack met and became close for a couple of reasons. To start, she was assigned the task of mentoring him when he first started working there. Also, Michelle and Barack were two of the few **minorities** working at the law firm, but also because she mentored him during his first experience working there. At the time, Michelle was focused on her career and not looking for a relationship, but she was impressed by Barack. Michelle and Barack

---

minority /mə-ˈnȯr-ə-tē/ noun 1: someone not old enough to be an adult 2: a part or number that is less than half of a whole 3: a group that makes up a smaller number of a larger group *<example: a minority population>*

both fell in love and married.

They have described their initial attraction to each other and an "opposites attract." Michelle was a stable, calm partner, and Barack was at first more adventurous. They married in 1992. A few years later, they tried to have children. Sadly, Michelle lost a baby during one pregnancy. After that, she decided to use a special medical procedure called *in vitro fertilization*, which helps women struggling to have a baby complete a pregnancy and give birth to a healthy baby.

Michelle and Barack Obama had two children together, two girls. The first child was named Malia Ann. She was born in 1998. The second child was named

Natasha. Natasha, also known as Sasha, was born in 2001.

Michelle and Barack Obama have stayed married for decades while having busy careers. Their marriage wasn't always perfect. They struggled and had many arguments during their early years as both worked in important jobs and Barack pursued a political career. Some of the arguments were about family and work life balance. They were both tired and stressed and had little time for conversations and quality time. However, they stayed together, worked it out and **persevered**.

---

persevere /ˌpər-sə-ˈvir/ verb: to keep trying to do something even though it is difficult <*example: persevere in the face of challenge*>

As of 2022, Michelle and Barack Obama continue to be married, work together and are building and managing multiple homes located in Washington D.C., Martha's Vineyard, which is in Massachusetts, and Hawaii.

CHAPTER 6
FUN FACTS

1. Hawaii is where the Obamas are now building a home, as of 2022. Did you know that Hawaii is the birthplace of surfing?

2. Martha's Vineyard is an island off the coast of Massachusetts on the east coast of the United States. The island was named after the daughter of the explorer, a British explorer named Bartholomew Gosnold who discovered the island in 1602.

CHAPTER 7
A LASTING LEGACY

Michelle Obama's lasting legacy is like a shining light that guides us towards kindness, health, and learning. When she was the First Lady of the United States, she cared a lot about children's health, making sure they eat good food and play to stay strong. Her "Let's Move!" campaign helped kids and families understand how important it is to be healthy.

Even after leaving the White House, Michelle keeps inspiring us. She wrote a special book called "Becoming" that tells her story and teaches us that no matter where we come from, we can become anything we want with hard work and belief in ourselves.

Michelle also believes in the power of education. She tells boys and girls all around the world that learning is like a superpower, and everyone deserves a chance to go to school and learn amazing things.

But most of all, Michelle Obama's legacy is about being kind, treating each other with respect, and working together to make our world better. She shows us that even small acts of kindness can create a big, positive impact. Her legacy reminds us to be the best version of ourselves and to always help others along the way.

GET SMART ABOUT MICHELLE OBAMA

INSPIRATIONAL QUOTES

Quotes are like magical words that can lift your spirits and make you feel like you can conquer the world! They are short and powerful sentences that carry big messages. Quotes come from inspiring people who have experienced many things in life. They teach us valuable lessons, remind us to be brave, and encourage us to follow our dreams. So, whenever you need some inspiration or a little boost of confidence, just read a quote, and you'll feel like you can achieve anything! Here are a few quotes from Michelle Obama to inspire you on your way!

> When they go low, we go high."

> Success isn't about how much money you make; it's about the difference you make in people's lives."

> The only limit to the height of your achievements is the reach of your dreams and your willingness to work hard for them."

> You may not always have a comfortable life, and you will not always be able to solve all of the world's problems at once, but don't ever underestimate the importance you can have."

> Choose people who lift you up."

> There is no limit to what we, as women, can accomplish."

> You don't have to be somebody different to be

important. You're important in your own right."

> Just do what works for you, because there will always be someone who thinks differently."

> We should always have three friends in our lives – one who walks ahead, who we look up to and follow; one who walks beside us, who is with us every step of our journey; and then, one who we reach back for and bring along after we've cleared the way."

" Do not bring people in your life who weigh you down. And trust your instincts ... good relationships feel good. They feel right. They don't hurt."

" Find people who will make you better."

" We need to do a better job of putting ourselves higher on our own 'to do' list."

" Failure is an important part of your growth and

developing resilience. Don't be afraid to fail."

❝ I am an example of what is possible when girls from the very beginning of their lives are loved and nurtured by people around them."

❝ One of the lessons that I grew up with was to always stay true to yourself and never let what somebody else says distract you from your goals. And so, when I hear about negative and false attacks, I really don't invest any energy in them, because I know who I am."

> Don't be afraid. Be focused. Be determined. Be hopeful. Be empowered."

> You might not always have a comfortable life, and you might not always be able to solve all of the world's problems at once, but don't ever underestimate the importance you can have."

> If you don't get out there and define yourself, you'll be quickly and inaccurately defined by others."

" Empower yourselves with a good education, then get out there and use that education to build a country worthy of your boundless promise."

" Instead of letting your hardships and failures discourage or exhaust you, let them inspire you. Let them make you even hungrier to succeed."

GET SMART ABOUT MICHELLE OBAMA

BOOK
DISCUSSION

How do you think that Michelle Obama's upbringing contributed to her success?

_____
_____
_____
_____
_____
_____

What other factors do you think contributed to Michelle"s success?

_____
_____
_____
_____
_____
_____

When Michelle Obama was a kid, she played sports a lot because her brother was her best friend and he loved sports. How do you think playing sports affected Michelle's choices and life later?

_____
_____
_____
_____
_____
_____
_____
_____

Michelle Obama often emphasizes the importance of empowerment and self-care. How do her messages about personal well-being relate to her passion for helping communities in need?

ADAM KENT

GET SMART ABOUT MICHELLE OBAMA

GLOSSARY

audio /'ȯ-dē-ˌō/ adjective: relating to sound *<example: audio equipment>*

charity /'kän-ˌtrakt/ noun 1: an organization focused on helping people in need *<example: donated to a charity>* 2: a gift intended to help people 3: goodwill toward people youth to get outdoors and exercise and stay healthy.

contract /'kän-ˌtrakt/ noun: an agreement, often legal, between two or more people or parties *<example: a work contract>*

corporate /'kȯr-p(ə-)rət/ adjective: relating to corporations, which are businesses that have been given by law that title and the rights that go with it <example: corporate America>

cultivate /'kəl-tə-ˌvāt/ verb: to raise and help grow with work and attention <example: cultivate corn or cultivate a friendship>

debilitating /di-'bi-lə-ˌtā-tiŋ/ noun: a force that is given to something that is spoken or written to draw attention to it <example: a debilitating fear>

designation /ˌde-zig-'nā-shən/ noun 1: an act of choosing to do something <example: designation of protected land> 2: a title or name that identifies something

discipline /'di-sə-plən/ noun: control that is gained through practice or insisting that rules be followed *<example: She gained discipline through practice.>* verb 1: punishment 2: a strict training meant to strengthen *<example: Teach discipline to a child.>*

documentary /ˌdä-kyə-'men-tə-rē/ noun: a film or a book dealing with factual events *<example: a documentary on whales>*

emphasis /'emfəsəs/ noun: a force that is given to something that is spoken or written to draw attention to it *<example: a special emphasis on learning>*

grounded / ˈgraun-dəd/ adjective: mentally and emotionally stable <example: *a grounded attitude*>

humble /ˈhəmbəl/ adjective 1: not regarding others as inferior 2: expressed without too much pride 3: low in condition or rank <example: *humble beginnings*>

induct /in-ˈdəkt/ verb: to admit as a member <example: *a induct into the Hall of Fame*>

minority /mə-ˈnȯr-ə-tē/ noun 1: someone not old enough to be an adult 2: a part or number that is less than half of a whole 3: a group that makes up a smaller number of a larger group <example: *a minority population*>

normalcy /ˈnȯr-məl-sē/ noun: the state of being normal or regular *<example: a return to normalcy after a terrible fight>*

organic /ȯr-ˈga-nik/ adjective: a type of food or beverage that is produced without the use of artificial chemicals *<example: organic food>* 2: related to living things

persevere /ˌpər-sə-ˈvir/ verb: to keep trying to do something even though it is difficult *<example: persevere in the face of challenge>*

prestigious /pre-ˈsti-jəs/ adjective: to have importance or respect that

is earned through excellence
<example: prestigious award>

SELECTED REFERENCES

Dance, Gabriel & Elisabeth Goodridge (October 7, 2009). "The Family Tree of Michelle Obama, the First Lady". The New York Times.

Finney, Ben; Houston, James D. (1996). "Appendix A - Hawaiian Surfing terms". Surfing - A History of the Ancient Hawaiian Sport. Rohnett, CA: Pomegranate Artbooks. pp. 94-97.

"First Lady Michelle Obama". whitehouse.gov. December 23, 2014.

Klar, Rebecca (April 27, 2020). "Michelle Obama documentary covering 'Becoming' book tour debuting on Netflix in May". The Hill.

"Michelle Obama Biography". National First Ladies' Library. February 5, 2009.

"Michelle Obama, Mia Hamm chosen for Women's Hall of Fame". The Philadelphia Inquirer. Associated Press. March 9, 2021.

"Michelle Obama Recalls Stressful Childhood in South Shore, at Whitney Young". DNA info. October 14, 2014.

Otterson, Joe (December 8, 2021). "'Upshaws' Co-Creator Regina Hicks Sets Netflix Overall Deal to Develop Comedy Series with Obamas' Higher Ground". Variety.

Slevin, Peter (March 18, 2009). "Mrs. Obama goes to Washington". Princeton Alumni Weekly.

Stolberg, Sheryl Gay (October 13, 2010). "Michelle Obama Hits Campaign Trail with Soft-Sell Message". The New York Times.

GET SMART ABOUT MICHELLE OBAMA

LETTER FROM THE AUTHOR

Dear Readers,

I hope you enjoyed this book and learned some take away that may help you as you continue to grow and make choices in life. Reading biographies of famous people can help us learn about ourselves and what decisions help and hurt people as they follow their dreams. If you enjoyed learning about this icon, you can read about more in our kids biographies series!

Happy learning and may your dreams come true!

All the best,
Adam Kent

GET SMART ABOUT MICHELLE OBAMA

COLLECT THE WHOLE
GET SMART BOOK SERIES

Here are just a few:

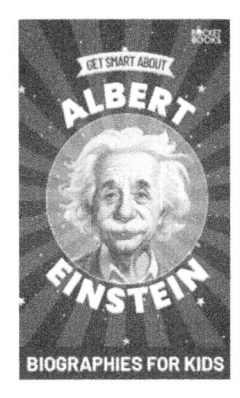

ROCKET BOOKS

Join our book club for free book offers. For more info email:

info@rocketkidsbookclub.com